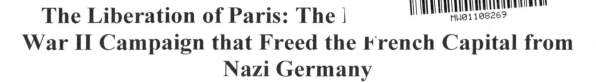

The Liberation of Paris: The I War II Campaign that Freed the French Capital from Nazi Germany

By Charles River Editors

A picture of French troops moving through Paris after the liberation

About Charles River Editors

Charles River Editors provides superior editing and original writing services across the digital publishing industry, with the expertise to create digital content for publishers across a vast range of subject matter. In addition to providing original digital content for third party publishers, we also republish civilization's greatest literary works, bringing them to new generations of readers via ebooks.

Sign up here to receive updates about free books as we publish them, and visit Our Kindle Author Page to browse today's free promotions and our most recently published Kindle titles.

Introduction

A picture of Charles de Gaulle and other French officers marching through Paris

The Liberation of Paris (August 1944)

"The hour of our great revenge has come." – Charles de Gaulle, August 1st, 1944

"People of Paris […] the long-awaited day has arrived! French and Allied troops are at the gates of Paris. It is the sacred duty of all Parisians to do battle! The hour of national resurrection has sounded." – poster displayed in Paris in August 1944

One of the most famous people in the world came to tour the city of Paris for the first time on June 28, 1940. Over the next three hours, he rode through the city's streets, stopping to tour L'Opéra Paris. He rode down the Champs-Élysées toward the Trocadero and the Eiffel Tower, where he had his picture taken. After passing through the Arc de Triomphe, he toured the Pantheon and old medieval churches, though he did not manage to see the Louvre or the Palace of Justice. Heading back to the airport, he told his staff, "It was the dream of my life to be permitted to see Paris. I cannot say how happy I am to have that dream fulfilled today." Four years after his tour, Adolf Hitler would order the city's garrison commander, General Dietrich von Choltitz, to destroy Paris, warning his subordinate that the city "must not fall into the enemy's hand except lying in complete debris." Of course, Paris was not destroyed before the Allies liberated it, but it would take more than 4 years for them to wrest control of France from Nazi Germany after they took the country by storm in about a month in 1940.

By the end of D-Day, June 6, 1944, the Allies had managed to successfully land 170,000 men, with over 75,000 on the British and Canadian beaches, 57,000 on the American beaches, and over 24,000 airborne troops. Thanks to Allied deception, the German army had failed to react to prevent the Allies from making the most of their landings. Just one division, the Hitlerjugend, would arrive the following day. Despite a fearsome and bloody day, the majority of the Allied forces had held their nerve, and most importantly, achieved their objectives. This ensured Operation Overlord was ultimately successful, and victory in Europe would be achieved within less than a year.

24 hours after the landings on June 6, 1944, however, the Allies still had plenty of work to do, and when the Allied High Command assessed the situation on the ground, it was clear that on no front had all of the objectives been achieved. The British and Canadians were ashore on Gold, Juno and Sword, yet Caen lay firmly in German hands. And in most cases, the various invasion forces lay clustered in isolated bands.

Given how the rest of the war played out, it's often forgotten that the British and Americans, after breaking out from their D-Day beachhead on the continent, did not free Paris from its Third Reich garrison. Instead, it was the people of Paris themselves, encouraged by the Allied armies putting the Germans to rout nearby, who retook the city, led by figures from the French Resistance. The revolt that emerged involved many factions, chiefly the followers of Charles de Gaulle, or the "Gaullists," and the communists of the PCF (Parti Communiste Francais, French Communist Party). These factions provided the spearhead and the catalyst sparking the people of Paris into rebellion against their Nazi masters, and the leadership coordinating that uprising and making it a success. Their rivalry and thirst for power spurred them on to outdo each other, but they all sought the same objective: defeat of the foreign occupiers.

Showing the mixed traits of a band of courageous freedom fighters and a bloodthirsty lynch mob, the Parisian rebels of 1944 also resembled the fiery, combative populace of medieval and Renaissance city-states. Though involving machine-guns, tanks, and radios, the liberation of Paris towards the end of World War II echoed the Sicilian Vespers or the Florentine street battles of the age of Girolamo Savonarola and the Medici.

The Liberation, once it began, required just one week to complete. Parisians fired the first shots on August 19, even as the Allies remained wary of trying to liberate Paris due to its cultural significance, knowing full well that Hitler could order the city destroyed. Nevertheless, on August 24, 1944, the French 2nd Armored Division began liberating parts of Paris, with overjoyed crowds of Parisians welcoming them, while the other Allies entered the eastern part of the city. General von Choltitz decided not to bomb Paris during a retreat, instead surrendering the city intact on August 25. That same day, Charles de Gaulle made a speech at the Hotel de Ville celebrating the freeing of the city and calling for French armies to sweep into Germany and exact "revenge" on the Germans. The newly liberated Parisians greeted his words, as might be expected, with a thunderous ovation.

As that response suggests, it's also conveniently forgotten that after the French people rose up to defeat the Germans in a patriotic frenzy worthy of opera, they subsequently turned on each other in a squalid outpouring of retribution, vendetta, and murder, sometimes of obviously innocent people. The torture and misogynistic abuse ended only when an official French government established itself firmly and cracked down on the anarchy, though it also carried out its own executions and imprisonments. The Allies' mistrust of all French factions as essentially authoritarian seemed vindicated.

The Liberation of Paris: The History of the World War II Campaign that Freed the French Capital from Nazi Germany chronicles the operations that pushed the Nazis out of Paris after nearly 4 years of occupation. Along with pictures of important people, places, and events, you will learn about the liberation of Paris like never before.

The Liberation of Paris: The History of the World War II Campaign that Freed the French Capital from Nazi Germany

Chapter 1: The French Resistance and the Allied Invasion of Europe

A picture of Hitler in Paris in 1940

The liberation of Paris gained its leadership and driving energy from the French Resistance, which consisted of dozens of independent groups, though Charles de Gaulle attempted to coordinate them from afar through the umbrella Conseil National de la Résistance (CNR) and the Forces Françaises de l'Intérieur (FFI). The Resistance numbered some 26,000 members in the Paris area in mid 1944, but only some 4,000 of these individuals possessed weapons. The PCF communists mustered the biggest "fighting unit," with some 600 men and women under arms, and de Gaulle cultivated their cooperation despite entertaining no desire to make France communist. In fact, he viewed his temporary Marxist allies as a totalitarian menace, but he wished to transcend political factions and act purely for France – and himself.

De Gaulle

One of the most important figures in the liberation, Henri Rol-Tanguy, frequently known by the pseudonym "Colonel Rol," headed the PCF in the region. A firebrand and convinced communist, Rol-Tanguy ultimately precipitated the Liberation, forcing the hand of his cautious Resistance colleagues. He also acted against the better judgment of de Gaulle and the Allied high command, but the events that came proved him right.

Colonel Rol

The Allied invasion force of 1944 included a contingent of Free French soldiers, many attached to Patton's spearheading Third Army. Of these, the 2e DB Free French 2nd Armored Division, under General Philippe de

Hauteclocque (known to history by his Resistance sobriquet of Philippe Leclerc), served a key role in liberating Paris, though its members remained unaware of this historic assignment until shortly before their tanks entered the City of Light.   Equipped with American uniforms, M1 rifles, M3 halftracks, M4 Sherman tanks, and other U.S. gear, the Frenchmen differed little in outward appearance from the other men of Patton's Third Army.

Leclerc

One other important individual in Paris, Swedish Consul General Raoul Nordling, acquired the odd distinction of serving as a vital neutral go-between for the Resistance and the Wehrmacht. The *Milwaukee Journal* published a dispatch from Bernard Kaplan on May 10th, 1958, when Nordling finally retired, in which the American reporter described the Swede as the "man who saved Paris" and stated, "French Communist Resistance fighters, who plotted to force the Germans to wage a major battle […] had no cause to thank the tall, taciturn Swede for thwarting them. To this day, many French Communists are convinced that, if Paris had been laid waste […] France would have emerged from the war with a Communist regime. […] [Nordling's] main task, as he saw it, was to persuade von Cholitz *[sic]* that nothing was to be gained by putting up a fight for Paris." (Kaplan, 1958, 8).

Nordling

The eventual liberation of the city took its character from many competing interests, including the restless ordinary Parisians, the communists offering aggressive focus and vigor through their wish for a revolutionary bloodbath, the restraining influence of several Gaullist leaders such as Alexandre Parodi, the tireless diplomatic efforts of Raoul Nordling, and the military discipline of the 2e DB Armored Division. One overriding goal – freeing Paris – welded these disparate factions into a victorious whole.

The biggest problem facing the leaders of the Allied nations was exactly when and where an invasion of

Europe should take place. At conferences in Casablanca and Tehran, 'The Big Three', Roosevelt, Churchill and Stalin, discussed the problem at length. It was clear to all that the Allies would have to force their way into Europe to have any hope of bring about the invasion of Germany. Up until 1943, the German defenders gave little thought to the potential for an allied landing of troops in Western Europe. At the same time, however, construction of Hitler's 'Atlantic Wall' continued, stretching from Norway in Northern Europe to France.

At that time, the German Army was more concerned with escaping its impending doom at the hands of the Russians in Stalingrad. This, coupled with the Allied invasion of Sicily and Italy, had still not woken Hitler to the prospect of a large scale invasion of France. Germany's apathy to the prospect of invasion is clear from the fact that German units were woefully underprepared for the upcoming Allied invasion. However, as Allied power grew through 1944, the Germans were forced to recognize that an invasion would be soon attempted. Under the command of Erwin Rommel, the German defenders of the French coast began serious efforts to shore up defenses in the areas around Pas de Calais and Normandy. Pillbox and bunker construction accelerated rapidly, millions of mines were laid and anti-landing devices were planted on the beaches of the region.

Entering 1944, France, once a lightly defended area, used largely for the recuperation of German soldiers from the Eastern front, was now the focus of Allied and German attention, with feverish plans made for the region on both sides. Reinforcements flooded into Northern France while tacticians planned for the impending invasion and counter-attack. The speed with which Germany had reinforced and strengthened the region meant that the Allies were less than certain of the success of the invasion. Britain, weary of amphibious landings after the disastrous Expeditionary Force campaign of 1940 came perilously close complete obliteration, was more than anxious. Allied military fortunes had been, at best, mixed. Professor Newton points out Britain, together with its continental allies, had lost its foothold in Europe but had managed to bloody the nose of Germany in the Battle of Britain in the summer of 1940. The Allies had lost Crete, yet stopped the Afrika Corps at El Alamein. With its American allies, Britain had successfully invaded Italy before becoming entangled in the costly German defense of the country. Britain, as a small island nation, lacked the manpower and supplies needed to singlehandedly defeat the German military. In comparison, the United States, an industrial colossus, had ample men and materials. Like Britain, American fortunes in the European theater were mixed, ranging from the successful landings in North Africa to the debacle of Kasserine Pass.

A sense of fear and foreboding marred the weeks and months in the build up to the invasion. Churchill was aghast at Eisenhower's bombing plan to accompany the landings, which would have resulted in the deaths of between 80,000 and 150,000 French civilians. It would have been an outrageous number of civilian casualties, and more French citizens killed by Allied bombing than had lost their lives in four years of German occupation. Churchill felt it was better to continue the bombing of Germany rather than inflict terrible casualties upon their French allies in support of what may be a doomed invasion. Just months before the planned invasion of France, Allied forces had landed at Anzio, just south of Rome. Almost immediately, the Allied landing force was halted and almost driven back into the sea. Churchill himself had been a leading player in the invasion of Gallipoli in 1915, a debacle which almost cost him his career. The idea of landing on the heavily defended Normandy coast filled Churchill with fear. On one occasion, just weeks before the launch of *Overlord,* the Prime Minister was heard to say, ""Why are we doing this? Why do we not land instead in a friendly territory, the territory of our oldest ally? Why do we not land in Portugal?"

Churchill was not alone. Many of the British military planners had felt a cross channel invasion "smacked of a seaborne Somme". Churchill had, however, persuaded the U.S. to give priority to the war in Europe, a position which caused many difficulties for Roosevelt. Pearl Harbor had outraged America and inflamed popular opinion against Japan, yet American attitudes towards Germany and Italy were far more ambivalent, due to the large proportion of American citizens with German or Italian heritage. However, at the somewhat bizarre Rattle Conference, described as a combination of intensive study and a 1920s themed house party, organized by Lord Louis Mountbatten, the assembled company settled upon Normandy as the invasion destination. Although further from Germany, it offered the Allies the chance to capture two major ports, Cherbourg and Le Harve.

By mid-1943, Hitler's Atlantic Wall looked formidable, with trenches, ditches, machine-gun nests, minefields, fortified artillery placements and bunkers. Over 8,000 such installations were operational, and 2,300 anti-tank guns and 2,700 guns larger than 75 mm were in place. However, Field-Marshall Gerd von Rundstedt, commander of the German forces in France, was still less than convinced of the strength of the Atlantic wall. He, along with many commanders in France, felt that the notion of an impenetrable Atlantic Wall was more of a figment of Hitler's imagination than a reality on the ground. Von Rundstedt argued that a static line defense such as the Atlantic Wall was only of use if there was defensible depth in the form of fall-back positions. Hitler, at the behest of von Rundstedt to reinforce France, sent Rommel to the area to shore up German defenses. Rommel oversaw the laying of millions of mines and underwater obstacles on the most likely landing beaches of the region, which was designed to keep the Allies from successfully landing ashore and driving the invasion force back into the sea. He wanted as much defenses as possible on the beaches, with infantry divisions as close as possible to landing sites and panzer divisions nearby to immediately strike at the landing forces.

Field Marshal Gerd von Rundstedt

A picture of German fortifications on D-Day. The countless small holes show the extent, and limited effect, of Allied shelling.

Even as the Atlantic Wall was strengthened, *Operation Fortitude* tricked Hitler into keeping 13 divisions in Norway rather than reinforcing the Normandy peninsula. It had also tricked German High Command into believing that 89 Allied divisions were preparing to land, with enough landing craft to bring 20 divisions ashore. In actuality, the figures were 47 and 6 respectively. Overreliance on intelligence crippled German defensive efforts in Normandy; it would not have taken a genius commander to realize that an exhausted Britain and a U.S. Army fighting a multi-theater war in the Pacific, Africa, Western Europe and Italy could not have fielded 87 divisions to attack Europe. Instead the Germans swallowed Allied misinformation hook, line and sinker. Statistics show the extent to which the German High Command was tricked by Allied deception plans. The Fifteenth Army, based at Pas de Calais, grew to a strength of 18 infantry and two panzer divisions. The Seventh Army, based in Normandy, had just 14 infantry and one panzer divisions. To make matters more complicated for the smaller force defending Normandy, the size of their theater of operations stretched for 995 miles of coastline. Rommel and von Rundstedt were both reminded of Frederick II's maxim, "He who defends everything, defends nothing."

Nevertheless, in facing these obstacles, it is perhaps best to consider what the alliance of millions of soldiers and support personnel were able to accomplish. On June 5, 1944, an armada of some 7,000 ships crossed the Channel towards the Normandy peninsula. Above it, 1,400 troop transports and 11,590 military aircraft of various types (along with 3,700 fighters) supported the landings. The following day, 175,000 soldiers were landed.

After the successful invasion on June 6, the Allies were left with a number of difficult tasks, most importantly capturing the critical port of Cherbourg and ensuring Allied forces were able to successfully link up before a push further east was made. Taking the town of Carentan was also of critical importance to the Allies, as the town was situated between the U.S. flanks. So important was the town that General Bradley was quite prepared to destroy every square inch of it if necessary.

Adding to the difficulties of taking the town was the fact that the German Army had blown up a bridge approaching the town. Engineers had moved material to repair the bridge but had failed to do so. The devout German 6th Parachute Regiment, which consisted of teenagers, held the territory immediately north of the town, which the U.S. intelligence thought had been abandoned. The 101st attack on the town began at 12.15 a.m. on June 11, with the 3rd Battalion of the 502nd Parachute Infantry leading the way. The soldiers dashed toward the bridge only to find that it had been unrepaired. Thus, the soldiers were forced to cross the river in a small boat, three at a time, until they reached an iron Belgian gate which the Germans had blocked the road with. As the gate would open just 18 inches, it forced the soldiers to squeeze through one by one. 50 yards past the gate lay the German paratroopers who poured machine gun fire and mortar rounds into the trapped Americans. Compounding the threat, two Luftwaffe fighters strafed and pounded the men, with I Company taking 25% casualties.

As the remaining Allied soldiers poured forward, with no chance of retreat, the situation seemed bleak. The remaining German paratroopers were embedded in a large farmhouse awaiting the U.S. assault. What they had not expected was for Colonel Robert Cole to, in a Medal of Honor winning assault, order his men to fix bayonets and charge the farmhouse. Due to the stress of battle, noise, fear or confusion, as Cole charged and turned to see his men, just 70 of his 250 men had followed his lead. Undeterred, Cole and his 70 men stormed the farmhouse, with the remainder of his troops frantically trying make up for their initial failings. Despite a fierce German resistance, Carentan fell to the Americans on June 12.

Churchill was not overstating the achievements of *Operation Overlord* when he described the plan "the greatest thing we have ever attempted". The greatest armada the world had ever seen had landed 170,000 soldiers on the heavily defended beaches of Normandy in just 24 hours. More remarkable was the fact that the operation was a success on every major level. Deception, tactical surprise and overwhelming force had contributed to the establishment of an adequate beachhead. Confusion and dissent had stopped the Germans massing for any great counterattack. The Atlantic Wall which Hitler had placed so much faith in had been breached, and the race to Paris was on.

Operation Overlord aimed to have the Allies reach the Seine River within 3 months of D-Day, and it's a testament to the men who fought and served on D-Day that the goal was reached early. To do so, the Allies overcame firm resistance from the Germans, atrocious weather that limited resupply for the Allies, and the difficult terrain of Normandy, which included endless hedgerows providing hidden cover. Moreover, the Allies reached their objective ahead of time despite the fact the objectives of D-Day were not entirely met; the Allies had not captured Caen, St-lo or Bayeux on the first day.

Chapter 2: Paris and Allied Strategy

The Allies sidelined Paris in a strategic sense for numerous reasons, planning to bypass it even before the July 24th breakout from the Normandy beachhead during Operation Cobra. Foremost among these loomed the concerns of damage to the city and the massive civilian casualties that would result from full-scale combat in its streets. Combat in the streets would unavoidably inflict tens of thousands of civilian deaths.

In a military sense, two pressing imperatives demanded an offensive past Paris rather than through it. First, the Allies needed to keep the pressure on the Germans to keep them off balance and prevent creation of a strong defensive line. Avoiding a repetition of World War I's static warfare assumed a high priority. Second, the western Allies recognized Stalin's Soviet Union for the violent, imperialistic dictatorship it was. Evidence of the

Katyn Forest Massacre and other grand-scale Soviet atrocities emerged only after the Soviets and the West allied to defeat Hitler. Nevertheless, the British and Americans prudently distrusted the Soviets' intentions, and all of them wanted the renown accruing to those capturing the Nazi capital. Churchill in particular expressed keen interest in taking Berlin as part of his insight that the Soviet Union presented no less threat to democracy in Europe than the Third Reich: "If they [the Russians] also take Berlin will not their impression that they have been the overwhelming contributor to our common victory be unduly imprinted in their minds, and may this not lead them into a mood which will raise grave and formidable difficulties in the future?"

Eisenhower asserted the Americans would also take Paris if the survival of its population depended on the action, such as to prevent starvation, for example. Indeed, the Parisians came very close to mass starvation, but the Americans lacked information about this until after the liberation began. Nazi Germany's communications blackout in conquered territories concealed the extent of the problem until the Parisians communicated directly with the Allies and Allied soldiers arrived in the city to report back to their commanders.

In any case, the Allies' supply situation barely enabled feeding their own armies on the continent. The offensive stopped in late summer and into autumn not due to German counterattacks, which General George S. Patton and other commanders defeated, but to logistical difficulties as the armies outpaced their supplies. Even supposing full cognizance of the Paris food situation – which the Allies lacked – they possessed insufficient food to satisfy the 2.5 million residents' hunger.

Patton

Ultimately, the Allies' decision to bypass Paris created a vital precondition for a successful popular rising. Had the Americans or British moved towards the sprawling metropolis in strength, the Germans would have immediately shifted large numbers of men into Paris in response. Providing a natural strong point nullifying the tremendous threat of Allied air power, Paris might have held up the Allied advance for months and inflict tens of thousands of casualties as the American and English soldiers fought for every block, street, and building with the experienced, rugged Wehrmacht infantry. During those months, of course, Hitler could raise fresh forces, build more tanks and aircraft, and prepare sturdier defenses along Germany's frontiers.

The Allies knew this clearly, and their commanders repeatedly asserted an aversion to turning Paris into "another Stalingrad." By avoiding the city, the Americans and British ensured the Germans left only a skeleton crew to garrison it. Thus, the German soldiers lacked the numbers to hold the metropolis against a popular uprising. Reinforcement of Paris by the Wehrmacht would make revolt impossible, but since the Germans saw no strategic value in bolstering the occupying forces, only French passivity that summer ensured the garrison's continued survival.

By July 1944, however, that passivity frayed rapidly as the Third Reich's strength visibly waned.

Chapter 3: Moving Towards Liberation

The D-Day landings both galvanized the Parisians with

fresh hope and starkly increased their hardships. Bombing raids in the suburbs, though often carried out at times and places the Allies hoped would avoid civilian casualties (such as factories on Sunday), proved inaccurate enough to kill hundreds of people regardless.

For the majority of those who lived in the City of Light, however, lack of food presented a far more omnipresent threat than bombs. The Allies struck at France's railway rolling stock mercilessly, destroying much of it. This produced the desired result of crippling German logistics, but it also deprived Paris of crucial food shipments and hampered refueling of Allied armies following the breakout from Normandy. The Germans confiscated most trucks to move their troops, further limiting civilian transport.

Paris failed to rise immediately after D-Day because the Parisians feared the Germans might crush the offensive. They listened eagerly (and illegally) to BBC news and propaganda broadcasts in French between 9:00 and 9:30 p.m. nightly, and the era's gallows humor reflected the twin obsessions of occupied Paris in 1944 – liberation and food: "[A] grim joke circulated around Paris that a Jew had killed a German soldier and eaten his heart at 9:20 PM. 'Impossible for three reasons,' ran the punch line: 'A German has no heart. A Jew eats no pork. And at 9:20 everyone is listening to the BBC.'" (Neiburg, 2012, 9).

For a time, the hope and defiance of the Parisians remained concealed for the most part. No proof yet existed in June 1944 that even Britain's newfound supporters, the Americans, could force a breakout in the teeth of the powerful, dreaded Wehrmacht. But as time passed and the Allied armies forced their way inland, the Germans proved impotent to contain them or push them back into the sea, and the city's inhabitants started defying the Nazis in ways they had not dared to during the Occupation. For example, the Nazis outlawed the French tricolor flag outside Vichy territory – where it appeared modified with fascist symbols – but in July, many people wore blue, white, and red garments, while women appeared in trios, with one member clad in each of the flag's three colors. These patriotic gestures came to a head on Bastille Day, July 14th, when a crowd bearing the French tricolor gathered in the Place Maubert. A small law enforcement detachment arrived to disperse the defiant celebrants, but they soon found themselves forced to turn tail, as a participant later described: "The [Parisian] police arrive. Someone cries: 'They are ten; we are ten thousand!' Faced with such resolve, the officers pulled back…At the Porte de Vanves, a bonfire was built, and Hitler was burned in effigy." (Rosbottom, 2014, 250).

While the French gathered courage, focus, and energy to launch the Liberation, the garrison's resolve steadily diminished. The initial occupying soldiers consisted of regular Wehrmacht infantry, who were tough, battle-ready, and efficient, but as the situation on the Eastern Front worsened, the German high command withdrew these troops for service in Russia and replaced them with poorly trained, poorly motivated second-line soldiers. These low quality infantry bullied the Parisians in the accustomed style, but they also appeared somewhat frightened by the millions of people they guarded. At times, the Wehrmacht men seemed to hide behind the French police and the collaborationist Milice (or militia). For example, during the period from mid-1943 through the Liberation, the German garrison "took security measures that appeared so extreme as to be laughable to Parisians; the sites where Germans assembled, previously lightly guarded, now were transformed into redoubts, even fortresses. Not only were barriers raised around even the smallest hotel, a special cadre of French police guarded them day and night; the detours that pedestrians had to take around these improvised bastions were wider." (Rosbottom, 2014, 243).

The German commander tasked with holding Paris, and the one who ultimately failed to put down the popular uprising that culminated with the liberation, brought a formidable reputation with him, but he only reached the city on August 9th, 10 days prior to the insurrection.

Dietrich von Choltitz, a Prussian nobleman, carried the sobriquet "The Beast of Sevastopol," thanks to his ferocious bombardment of that city. Deceptively mild in appearance – with a bland, plump face, slicked hair, and a monocle – von Choltitz found himself tasked by Hitler with holding Paris at all costs or destroying it before the Allies could liberate the metropolis. Though both friend and enemy thought him a deadly leveler of cities, von Choltitz proved extremely circumspect and may have spared Paris partial annihilation on at least two occasions.

Von Choltitz

As summer 1944 continued, the Parisians grew more intransigent, the Allies landed in Normandy, and the July 20th bomb plot failed to kill the Fuhrer, leading to grim scenes of purge, suicide, and execution. Nevertheless, the German occupiers maintained a curious level of what passed for normality in their relations with the French. Horse races continued up to July 31st, along with art exhibitions and auctions, operas, plays, and 91 concerts in June alone. At the same time, the increasing disruptions to public life thanks to food shortages and periodic loss of electric power caused skirmishing in the streets, the murder of some Milice members and officials, and arrests by the Germans (followed by torture and maiming of the French prisoners rounded up). The Germans themselves provided a crisp statistical analysis of the Parisians' plight: "Occupation authorities calculated that nutrition in France, on a par with Germany in pre-war years, had sunk drastically: the average daily intake of a Frenchman was 1,462 calories versus 2,352 in Germany, about 38 percent less. Already plagued by shortfalls in coal supplies and electrical current, Parisians in particular were adversely affected." (Mitchell, 2008, 110).

Among the Nazi supporters, the Paris police had an extremely delicate position. These collaborators, who often had little choice between continuing their collaboration and death, clearly understood the Third Reich's disintegrating condition by summer 1944. Many of the police intended to side with the liberators when Liberation arrived, hoping in this way to gain a de facto pardon from their fellow citizens. However, if a rebellion occurred, it needed to be sufficiently large to offer a high probability of success before the police could safely support it. Backing a failed revolt would cost them their lives, possibly under highly unpleasant circumstances in a Gestapo torture chamber. In fact, the Resistance covertly informed the police that those policemen opposed to the Germans ought to keep their jobs and from August 1943 onward, the Nazis noted that the Paris police seemed to do little against the Resistance or even random citizens expressing hate and outrage towards the occupiers.

The police effort against the Bastille Day celebrants on July 14th exhibited such feeble commitment to actually breaking up the demonstration – and the brief but defiant labor strikes that followed – that the crowd shouted "the police are with us!" The spur-of-the-moment popular reaction proved nearly correct. The Bastille Day celebrations, in fact, tested the waters of police attitude and revealed that law enforcement no longer sided with the Germans or the Vichy government for the most part. While some police arrested people and one squad killed Yves Toudic, a trade union captain, with gunshots, others sang the Marseillaise and even protected the populace from the Vichy militia, or Milice, as the Jewish hairdresser Albert Grundberg reported in a diary entry: "I heard the sounds of the 'Marseillaise' being sung by hundreds and hundreds of people. […] Mme Oudard […] came to see me, draped with a huge tricolour flag,

like most of the passers-by. She told me it had been magnificent and that there had been demonstrations all over Paris. Policemen followed the demonstrators and warned them when the Milice threatened to get too close." (Cobb, 2013, 19-20).

Dietrich von Choltitz, the newly appointed Wehrmacht governor of the city on the Seine, soon proved to have a bark much worse than his bite. Despite his formidable reputation, the German – through a mix of deep self-interest, war-weariness, and perhaps even a smattering of disinterested unwillingness to damage so important a European cultural center – blustered and postured but took little action to suppress the growing patriotic fervor of the Parisians. Upon his arrival in Paris, von Choltitz offered a spectacle of strength intended to deter his new charges from rash actions. He organized a large portion of his garrison into a parade involving infantry, artillery, and both armored and soft-skinned vehicles on the Avenue de l'Opera, and these men and machines marched in a loop through nearby streets, creating the impression of an endless stream of armed might goose-stepping by the spectators. The wily Beast of Sevastopol watched his stratagem from the comfort of a cafe.

If von Choltitz hoped to overawe the French, however,

this display failed. Indeed, the German commander summed up his actual reluctance to employ unrestrained force in his new command with a pithy phrase spoken even before he lost the city to its citizens: "Paris is like a beautiful woman; when she slaps you, you don't slap her back."

By the end of July, the Resistance's most formidable opponents consisted of the fascist Milice. This paramilitary force of right-wing fanatics, heavily armed and led in the Paris region by Max Knipping, had none of the submerged patriotism of the police, nor the wily circumspection and restraint of von Choltitz. Always ready to kill, Knipping's men responded to the Bastille Day demonstrations by summarily executing 28 prisoners at Sante Prison. They continued to murder Resistance members and anyone suspected of assisting them even as the possibility of liberation loomed nearer daily. The growing neutrality of the police and the waning of Wehrmacht strength left a power vacuum the Milice eagerly occupied, using intimidation, torture, violence, and execution to build their influence with the same brutal energy as Hitler's Brownshirts and Mussolini's Blackshirts in the 1930s.

Knipping

Nonetheless, many factors tipped Paris rapidly in the
direction of revolt in August 1944. The approach of the
Allies and defeat of the Wehrmacht in northern France
played a major role, as did the misery of reduced food.
The increasingly sympathetic attitude of the police to
those who flaunted their patriotic feelings provided great
encouragement. Moreover, the Germans steadily drew
down their numbers, while von Choltitz communicated
notable unwillingness to crush the Parisians too
vigorously despite his swaggering bravado. Against this
backdrop, the Milice appeared as intolerable hooligans or

jackals picking over the carcass of the occupation rather than as terrifying enforcers of an unassailable fascist order. All events and popular impressions, in short, flowed together into a gathering avalanche of rebellion against the invader.

The rumblings of incipient revolt remained fairly restrained for some time due to the military situation. Though Hitler's armies failed to prevent the D-Day landings on June 6th and his bungled deployment of panzers in dense coastal terrain failed to dislodge the American and British beachhead, the Wehrmacht remained formidable for some time after the invasion. Fighting with skill, courage, and elan, the soldiers of the Third Reich temporarily contained the Allies in Normandy. The situation could not last, however. The average American soldier proved a tough and resourceful opponent in turn, and the dominance of the skies by the excellent P-38 Lightning, P-47 Thunderbolt, and P-51 Mustang aircraft of the U.S. Air Force provided a devastating solution to remaining concentrations of Wehrmacht and Waffen SS armor. Additionally, the arrival of the Third Army, led by the unstable but keenly aggressive Patton, spelled the end of the Wehrmacht's delaying action.

Double disaster struck the German command towards the end of July. The abortive July 20th assassination plot against Adolf Hitler led to a brutal purge and confusion in the Wehrmacht's middle and upper echelons as the Fuhrer attempted to ferret out traitors. On July 24th, the Americans launched Operation Cobra to break out of the beachhead area. Bogged down for a day by the last flare-up of German resistance, the U.S. Army forces soon burst through the crumbling German defenses.

On July 25th, U.S. Army General J. Lawton Collins unleashed the 2nd and 3rd Armored Divisions, punching through the German lines and effecting a massive breakout. Supported by clouds of fighter-bombers and heavy bombers that carpet-bombed any areas of resistance, the Americans soon revealed the frailty of the forces opposing them. The elite Panzer Lehr Division, caught in the direct path of the attack, suffered 70% casualties, prompting its commander, Fritz Bayerlein, to report in a despairing rage: ""Out in the front everyone is holding out […] Everyone. My grenadiers and my engineers and my tank crews—they're all holding their ground. Not a single man is leaving his post. Not one! They're lying in their foxholes mute and silent, for they are dead. Dead! Do you understand? You may report to the Field Marshal that the Panzer Lehr Division is annihilated." (Mitcham, 2000, 91).

General Omar Bradley and Collins (right)

Patton and the Third Army arrived on August 1st, and the 2e DB Free French 2nd Armored Division under General Philippe Leclerc, attached to the Third Army, landed in France on the same day. Patton, sensing an opportunity, persuaded Bradley and Eisenhower to allow him to push through the disintegrating Germans towards the Seine and the German border itself. Like earlier Wehrmacht successes with Blitzkrieg, this strategy encircled large numbers of Germans, forcing the surrender of tens of thousands and placing the rest at a huge disadvantage.

The Wehrmacht's fortunes sank lower as the U.S. Seventh Army landed in the Riviera under the command of Lieutenant General Jacob Devers on August 15th. This attack, Operation Dragoon, tore into the soft underbelly of German resistance. The 1st Airborne Task Force made a foray into Italy near Menton, the superbly picturesque resort town dubbed the Pearl of France, while the rest of the Seventh Army and the Free French First Army sliced northward, enveloping German forces from the south even as Patton encircled them from the north.

Devers

Patton's Third Army assisted most directly with the liberation of Paris. Operating just north of the city, the aggressive American army, spearheaded by the 4th Armored Division (known to the Germans as "Roosevelt's

Butchers") with its M4 Sherman tanks and deadly M18 Hellcat tank destroyers, disrupted Wehrmacht formations that might otherwise have entered Paris. Additionally, it had the 2e DB Free French Armored Division with it, bringing the hard-fighting unit within a close jump of Paris. This proximity led to the deployment of the 2e DB Division to aid the liberation. Patton's ferocious penetration of German lines would place Leclerc's men within striking distance of their nation's former capital at precisely the correct moment.

Chapter 4: The Start of the Liberation

Encouraged by the Allies' presence on the continent – especially after several attempts to dislodge them ended with hundreds of German armored vehicles pulverized by relentless fighter-bomber attacks – the French stepped up the shooting of collaborators steadily throughout June, July, and early August. No reprisal executions deterred the Resistance, as the Communists of the PCF welcomed the chance of a violent "proletarian revolution" and the rest of the Resistance maintained a high level of defiance towards the Nazis.

After the Bastille Day celebrations on July 14th, a strike by railway workers followed the Milice revenge murders at Sante prison. The 28 men killed included many railroad employees, prompting this strike by some of the city's most vital service providers. Without rail service, food deliveries ceased and distribution of other necessities grew difficult. These hardships enraged the Parisians further against the German occupiers. The Germans themselves, feeling the pinch of hunger, also suffered directly from the strikes.

On July 20th, the sight of Germans turning on Germans heartened the astonished Parisians, who knew nothing of the bomb-blast in the faraway Wolf's Lair headquarters of Adolf Hitler. The Wehrmacht deployed both infantry and tanks to arrest a minimum of 1,200 SS men and Gestapo, believing Hitler dead. When the news that the Fuhrer survived reached Paris, the Wehrmacht released their prisoners, proclaiming the incident a drill. The French, however, knew better, and propaganda leaflets appeared crowing at the divisions in the Teutonic ranks. Despite this loss of unity, the Germans continued rounding up Jews, filling up July's monthly quota of a thousand for Paris with 327 children and 27 infants, most of whom died in gas chambers in Germany or Poland.

Fearing the destruction of the Reich, some German soldiers began planning desertion by purchasing civilian clothes, but the French noticed the foredoomed nature of this effort. The 38% difference in caloric intake between the occupiers and the conquered meant that the Germans all appeared smooth and fleshy next to the lean, hollow-cheeked, angular French. A German in civilian clothes stood out among the Parisians as clearly as though he still wore his Feldgrau uniform. The large numbers of German women brought into the city during the Occupation to fill clerical, messenger, medical, and lower-level administrative roles also began a mass exodus at this time. The French noted the departure of these "gray mice," as they nicknamed the Teutonic women, as a hopeful sign, indicating the Germans had little expectation of holding the city. Many male German bureaucrats and administrators fled with them, as wryly noted by the satirical diarist Jean Galtier-Boissière: "Along the rue Lafayette, coming from the luxury hotels around the Étoile, sparkling torpedoes pass by containing purple-faced generals, accompanied by elegant blonde women, who look as if they are off to some fashionable resort." (Beevor, 2007, 32).

Charles de Gaulle attempted control of the Resistance and any liberation efforts from afar. On June 13th, he landed near Bayeax and made an impassioned speech at the town, during which he played down the role of the Allies in freeing France. From there, he boarded his vessel again and left French shores temporarily, first meeting with President Roosevelt and then establishing his headquarters at Algiers. The tall Frenchman – known jocularly as "the Great Asparagus" due to his height –

used the radio facilities of this North African fastness to broadcast increasingly belligerent messages across France.

Despite his calls to resistance, the Gaullists among the FFI factions sought restraint in the actions taken against the Germans. The Communists, on the other hand, remained fiercely active, almost seeming determined to provoke a brutal reaction from the Germans. As the best-armed of the factions, the PCF under Henri Rol-Tanguy possessed the means to exercise this aggression, but they lacked the police support the Gaullists enjoyed.

Meanwhile, the German soldiers, frequently ambushed during July by small, furtive bands of Resistance fighters, grew jumpy, so the situation remained dangerous for the French also. Though most Wehrmacht vehicles fought elsewhere, von Choltitz commanded a small force of tanks to supplement his riflemen, as the Polish exile Andrzej Bobkowski noted on a warm evening in early August: "The sun has set; night is falling. The black towers of Notre Dame stand out against a pink sky that shimmers and changes colour. […] There is a grinding sound from the street as a steel giant goes by, covered with tree branches. It is a solitary German Tiger tank […] Blue flames burst from its massive exhausts, sending sparks into the sky." (Cobb, 2014, 39).

Besides tanks, von Choltitz's garrison also mustered artillery, halftracks, machine-guns, and bomber support from a Luftwaffe detachment stationed at a nearby airfield. Nevertheless, the Germans remained relatively quiescent despite the rising tide of French defiance. Living in a Paris apartment, Pablo Picasso even found enough peace to paint a series of pictures showing the maturation of a potted tomato.

Chapter 5: Full Boil

A German decision in the second week of August finally sparked the Parisians into full-scale rebellion against the occupation. On the 13th of August, the distant, rattling echo of heavy weapons fire drifted into the city on the western breeze, indicating the Allied advance's closeness. The circumstance drew more comment from the French than von Choltitz's largely ignored military parade the day before on August 12th.

The French Resistance feared that the thousands of prisoners in German hands might be slaughtered if the Allies broke through or an uprising occurred in the city. However, true to form, they could not agree on a rescue plan. Dithering and squabbling, the factions eventually deferred to de Gaulle's lieutenant on the scene, Parodi. Parodi did exactly nothing, deeming any action too "risky," but he sent a message to Eisenhower suggesting the American commander threaten those who killed prisoners with war crimes trials after their capture. This utterly impotent response doubtless helped compel the communist Colonel Rol-Tanguy and his PCF to act unilaterally when the opportunity to launch a rebellion arrived.

Parodi

The hated Milice under Max Knipping provided the final push towards open revolt. On the morning of August 13th, 1944, the Germans and Milice disarmed and arrested the local police units in a trio of northern Parisian suburbs. Resistance leaders meeting at that moment at the Rue Vulpian took great alarm at this news. The Paris police, numbering some 20,000, constituted the best-armed answer to von Choltitz's 16,000 low-quality garrison troops, and if the Germans disarmed them, only some 2,000 to 4,000 armed Resistance members remained to oppose the occupiers and the Milice. Police disarmament spelled the end of any hope the city might liberate itself. In 1940, Britain's gun control policy had disarmed its populace so effectively that only a donation of 5,000 rifles from the United States provided weapons to the Home Guard in the face of invasion, and the French similarly lacked private firearms to resist an invader. Max Knipping grasped this fact clearly. As part of his Milice power play, in which the Milice would supplant all regular police to keep order – and impose fascist regimentation on society – Knipping ordered the police leadership to disarm all uniformed gendarmes under their command.

The police, with their Resistance sympathies and fear of reprisals from the victors, found themselves faced with a conundrum. Their first step on the 13th consisted of withdrawing all police officers from the streets and ordering them to don ordinary daily attire, thus making it extremely difficult for the Milice or Germans to identify and disarm them. Representatives of the three main police

Resistance groups met on August 14ᵗʰ, and PCF leader Colonel Rol-Tanguy also attended the meeting. The day's sweltering, stifling weather seemed a presage of the ominous events soon to unfold in the city. The Front National member noted that if the police aided the Resistance by striking to prevent their disarmament, their collaborationist record would likely be forgotten. The Gaullist Honeur et Police expressed eagerness to begin casting off German rule, but the representative of the third police resistance faction – the Police et Patrie – demurred out of basic fear of the Germans.

At this moment, Rol-Tanguy rose to speak. The tough, energetic, handsome communist simply reminded the gathered police officials that the FFI called on the French to stop working for the Germans. This simple, direct statement persuaded the men, and they agreed unanimously to call a police strike the following day. Before midnight, leaflets printed by the Police et Patrie reached every gendarmerie station in the city with a simple order: "No police officer shall allow himself to be disarmed or become the target of any coercive measure whatsoever."

The following morning, no policemen appeared on the Paris streets. According to police records, 95% of the morning shift declined to come to work, supporting the massive strike. Even more crucially, the police cleared their weapons from the stations the night before, hiding them in regular homes and businesses around the city where the Germans could not easily or quickly locate them. Thus, police armories across Paris stood empty on the morning of August 15th.

Amedee Bussiere, the collaborationist Prefect of Police, exhorted a group of gendarmes to return to duty in the afternoon, but the men ignored him. Von Choltitz moved the curfew forward by an hour and sent 3,000 political prisoners east by cattle car to die in Buchenwald concentration camp as punishment for the strike, but he privately used the Swedish consul Raoul Nordling to ask Parisian officialdom to keep the city running as best as possible, promising "Paris would be neither defended nor destroyed, nor delivered to looting and arson." (Zaloga, , 54).

As a result, a bizarre truce was developed by Nordling as he shuttled back and forth between the enemies, and it held for several days: "[O]ne witness noticed that German trucks would pass others filled with Resistance fighters, neither glancing at the other for fear that a firefight might explode into a major conflagration. Rather incredibly, and certainly suddenly, it seemed that the Occupation was ending quickly and more peacefully than had been hoped." (Rosbottom, 2014, 253).

No single individual or organization controlled the Paris liberators, however. Mere negotiation between administrators could not restrain every faction of the Resistance or the people of Paris themselves. Furthermore, the success of the police strike inspired others to follow suit; the railway workers, electrical workers, postal workers, telephone and telegraph personnel, and subway employees all went on strike on the 15th or 16th, to the point that 60% of Paris' workforce refused to do their jobs while the Germans remained.

Meanwhile, Nordling attempted to secure the release of the political prisoners being sent east in cattle cars to torture, starvation, and death in Himmler's camps, but without avail. A few prisoners managed to break away and escape, while others were shot while seeking to flee or grappling with their guards. Two-thirds of those crammed into the cattle-cars, including 168 captured Allied airmen, died of abuse, overwork, malnutrition, disease, or outright execution before war's end. Nevertheless, they too had caught the spirit of liberation, and a rare moment when history achieved something of the character of tragic opera followed. As the cattle cars, packed with suffering humanity – dehydrated, hungry, trapped in their own waste after being locked inside all day under the August sun – rolled down the rails towards the east that night under an approaching thunderstorm, the

Gestapo guards on the platform heard the muffled voices of several thousand men and women swelling from inside, defiantly singing the Marseillaise: "To arms, citizens, Form your battalions! We march, we march! Let impure blood Water our furrows!"

Peace frayed swiftly in the city despite the superb weather that followed the thunderstorms, the efforts of Nordling, and the general passivity of von Choltitz. News of the Allied landings in the south – first by the American 1st Airborne Task Force parachuting into Menton, then by the Free French First Army landing all along the Riviera coast – reached Paris almost immediately thanks to the BBC. The French took fire, while Adolf Hitler remarked that the day of the landings represented the worst day of his life.

Germans and Resistance fighters skirmished with each other from the 15th-18th, dotting the Paris streets with corpses. A French policeman, 27 year old Louis Bretlivet, used his pistol to shoot and kill two Gestapo men attempting to arrest a Jewish family, before the other Germans riddled him fatally with bullets. Elsewhere in the city, the diarist Odette Lainville observed, in surreal contrast, dozens of young French men peddled bicycles rapidly around the streets, their girlfriends perched on the handlebars to enjoy the superlative weather. Other youths, both male and female, enthusiastically built barricades across the roads – which the German tanks plowed through with ease – and prepared Molotov cocktails for the day of action.

The communist PCF met on August 16th and decided to launch a revolt on August 19th, with or without the support of the other Resistance factions. However, Colonel Rol-Tanguy decided to give the other parties the chance to join in. In particular, he wanted the cooperation of Parodi's Gaullists. Though Rol-Tanguy despised de Gaulle himself, he knew the numerous, well-armed police listened mainly to Parodi, and without them, the planned Liberation stood little chance of success.

The Gestapo fled the city on August 17th, knowing the French and the Allies would extend little mercy to them. They even carried away their desks, chairs, and instruments of torture as they evacuated in trucks along the eastward roads. Other Germans crowded the trains still running to Germany, sensing the metropolis' dangerously hostile mood.

On August 18th, the leaders of the main Resistance factions met in Vanves. Rol-Tanguy's communists, busy as ever with their clandestine printing presses, already worked to galvanize the city with a fresh leaflet: "Organize yourselves neighborhood by neighborhood. Overwhelm the Germans and take their arms. Free Great

Paris, the cradle of France! Avenge your martyred sons and brothers. Avenge the heroes who have fallen for…the freedom of our   Fatherland… Choose as your motto: A BOCHE [Kraut] FOR EACH OF US. No quarter for these murderers! Forward! Vive la France!"

At the meeting itself, the Gaullist leaders, especially Parodi, urged caution and repeated their typical arguments. Rol-Tanguy, however, forced their hand by declaring the communists would launch a rebellion the following day with or without the help of the other Resistance factions, relying on the people of Paris to assist. Parodi, realizing the wrath of the Germans would fall on the Parisians and all of the Resistance whether they participated or not, agreed to assist. He also wished to maintain a strong Gaullist element in whatever power structure emerged from the rebellion, rather than acquiescing to a unilateral communist coup. Rol-Tanguy, on the other hand, badly needed Parodi's police support, and he possessed sufficient pragmatism to accommodate the Gaullists in order to obtain it. Thus, the two factions agreed to cooperate in raising the city against the Germans on the morrow.

August 19th brought the start of the liberation in dramatic fashion. For all his fire and drive, the police and Gaullists beat Rol-Tanguy to the punch; riding a bicycle through the Ile de la Cite in the fresh, sunny coolness of the summer morning shortly after sunup, the Colonel passed the huge Prefecture of Police building, the central headquarters of Paris' 16,000-20,000 strong police force. To his astonishment, the sound of the Marseillaise rolled out of the windows as he passed, sung by hundreds of male voices. Rol-Tanguy approached the door and found it guarded by armed policemen in civilian clothes, wearing FFI brassards. The men turned him away curtly, but the resourceful Resistance leader pedaled a short way, found a secluded corner, and changed into his Spanish Civil War uniform, which he carried in a pannier on his bicycle. When the police saw his crisp military garments, they saluted and allowed him to enter.

Inside, Rol-Tanguy found that the once-reluctant Parodi had stolen a march on him. At dawn, 2,000 Gaullist policemen descended on the Prefecture, led by a handsome, blond police officer in his 20s named Yves Bayet. Bayet used a car in front of the building as an impromptu podium, from which he bellowed, "In the name of General de Gaulle and the Provisional Government of the French Republic, I take possession of the Prefecture de Police!" The policemen arrested the collaborationist prefect Amedee Bussiere, later sentenced to life imprisonment but released in 1951, two years before his death. Yves Bayet then brought the Gaullist Charles Luizet to the Prefecture in a black Citroen from the cafe where he waited, and the police acclaimed Luizet the new Prefect.

Rol-Tanguy found a sort of council of war underway inside the Prefecture. Parodi, present among the many men gathered there, rose to address the police and others. "He had just begun to speak when André Tollet, the head of the Paris Liberation Committee, interrupted him. Tollet accused Parodi of having started the insurrection prematurely [...] Colonel Rol-Tanguy leaped in, shouting 'Paris is worth two hundred thousand dead!'" (Argyle, 2014, 180).

Now determined on action, Parodi abandoned caution and worked to make the rebellion successful. Though he deeply distrusted the communists' ultimate intentions, he recognized the fighting spirit and valuable experience of Colonel Rol-Tanguy. As the meeting cooled from its initial argument, Parodi ordered the entire Resistance mobilized for action and gave Rol-Tanguy command over all Resistance forces in the city. After doing so, he remarked bleakly, "If I have made a mistake I shall have a lifetime to regret it in the ruins of Paris."

For his part, Rol-Tanguy acted quickly. The communists, well-prepared thanks in large measure to his intelligence and furious energy, already had a list of 80 key positions to seize before the end of the first day, and bands of

Resistance fighters moved rapidly through the streets to occupy these places. The Gaullists, still distrusting the communists, sent their own trusted fighters and police to take the Hotel de Ville and several other prestigious targets.

The sound of skirmishing in the streets alerted von Choltitz of the rebellion even before telephone calls told him of the Prefecture's seizure. The Beast of Sevastopol took the news calmly and ordered some of his men to retake the Prefecture. Nevertheless, the Germans showed little haste and only arrived near the police headquarters at 3:00 p.m. A group of SdKfz 251 Hanomag halftracks arrived first in the Boulevard du Palais, disgorging approximately 50 men of the Sicherungs Regiment 5. These men shot out every window on the street, carrying out "reconnaissance by fire" for French snipers. Then, with a terrific roar of engines and creaking and groaning of tracks, von Choltitz's lone Panzer VI Tiger rolled onto the scene. Its first shot blew down the gates into the Prefecture courtyard, and the second shell smashed into the building but punched right through. The German gunner loaded AP (armor-piercing) rounds rather than HE (high explosive) for reasons that remain unclear.

The Tiger I then departed, and more halftracks arrived carrying additional infantry. Two captured, repainted Renault R-35 tanks with 37mm guns accompanied them, with a third tank, possibly a Panzer V Panther (though Allied and Resistance troops alike tended to identify all German tanks as the lethal Panther or Tiger variants). The police only had Molotov cocktails to use as anti-tank weapons, but of a new, improved sort. "[T]he Molotov cocktail had progressed [...] to a safer contraption using liquid acid mixed with the gasoline and a small packet of dry chemical on the outside which ignited the gasoline when the bottle was smashed. The famous scientist and political activist Frédéric Joliot-Curie, son-in-law of the legendary Madame Curie, undertook the manufacture of these refined Molotov cocktails." (Zaloga, 2008, 58).

The initially overconfident Germans drove their tanks close under the Prefecture's walls, only to have a policeman on the roof hurl a well-aimed Molotov cocktail straight into the open hatch of one of the R-35s. A blinding fountain of flame erupted from the hatch as the improvised incendiary grenade killed the crew and knocked out the tank. The other two tanks drew back immediately and continued to fire relatively ineffective AP rounds at the building, holing its walls here and there but doing little more.

Late in the afternoon, von Choltitz ordered a Luftwaffe strike on the Prefecture, but the German airmen deemed the hour too late for an attack in such a densely populated area. The Sicherungs Regiment pulled back, ending the hours-long firefight that left 40 Wehrmacht soldiers dead and 70 more wounded. The police and the Resistance elsewhere in the city suffered losses of 125 killed and approximately 500 wounded on the 19th.

After the day's events, the police began doubting their ability to hold the Prefecture. Despite knocking out a tank and capturing new weapons from several halftracks, nightfall found their ammunition practically exhausted, though Molotov cocktails remained abundant. At this point, the ever-busy Raoul Nordling came to their rescue. Nordling appeared at von Choltitz's headquarters (the Hotel Meurice) even while fighting continued at the Prefecture late in the afternoon of the 19th. Shuttling back and forth between Luizet and von Choltitz, the Swedish consul slowly hammered out a sort of truce despite the intransigence of the French and von Choltitz's brutal bluster.

As a first step, von Choltitz recognized the FFI and Resistance as regular soldiers, giving them nominal protection from summary execution as terrorists. The police and Germans also agreed not to shoot at each other. Though the police knew nothing at the time, this prevented a massive combined tank attack and Luftwaffe airstrike on the Prefecture von Choltitz had slated for the morning of August 20th. This achievement of Nordling likely saved the lives of the 2,000 men defending the

Prefecture.

While the truce held after a fragile fashion in some areas, the Resistance and Germans continued shooting at each other throughout the rest of Paris, but the truce gradually took hold on the 20th, despite continued bloody incidents. Rather than directed fighting, random violence marked the day of the truce. Both the Germans and the Resistance proved trigger-happy and nervous, firing wildly at the slightest sign of danger, real or imagined. The SS also viciously executed some French police in their custody, some of whom died with dapper composure that elicited admiration from the onlookers.

In one bizarre incident, the Germans arrested Parodi himself, bringing him face to face with von Choltitz. The German discussed the situation quite civilly with the man who, in effect, represented his French opposite number. He asked if Parodi wanted food released from the German supply depots, to which the Frenchman responded that "the Parisians have been hungry for the past four years; they can put up with starving for another four days." (Cobb, 2013, 183). Von Choltitz released the Frenchman and his two companions, and Parodi refused to shake the Wehrmacht general's hand while leaving.

Several groups of German soldiers surrendered to the Parisians during the day or asked French police to arrest them. The Germans lost 12 men as prisoners and one Renault R-35 tank when a crowd of 500 Parisians surrounded the vehicle at Batignolles. The Germans, unwilling to fire on the crowd or attempt to run them over, tried unsuccessfully to push away the men and women clambering onto their vehicle, and after an hour or two, they simply surrendered. The crowd marched them to the nearest police station and appropriated the armored vehicle for FFI use.

Though the leaders of both sides attempted to enforce the truce, lack of communications led to continued street fighting throughout August 21st. The French, as in every revolution since the 18th century, busily constructed barricades at every chokepoint in the Paris streets. Soon, approximately 600 barricades dotted the City of Light, many defiantly crowned with tricolor, American, or Soviet flags stitched together out of clothing scraps by the neighborhood's women.

The Germans entered a state of siege by the 22nd. Without collaborators or the police supplying them with information, they had little idea of major developments in the city, and due to constant sniping, the Germans only patrolled inside their SdKfz 250 and 251 Hanomag halftracks, which provided shelter from small arms fire.

While many Parisians gathered as spectators to the

skirmishes, others ignored the fighting completely. Men and women basked in the warm August sun, conserving energy, while fishermen in canvas chairs dotted the banks of the Seine, ignoring panzers and halftracks roaring by as they relaxed and waited for a bite. Parisian women displayed as much indifference to the situation as the men, sometimes walking through marching groups of belligerent Germans as though the Wehrmacht were ordinary market crowds. Adding to the surreal air, the violent standoff came to an end at dinnertime as both the Resistance and Germans abandoned the day's positions in search of food.

Away to the west, however, important events occurred at the headquarters of the American Third Army. Sent by Colonel Rol-Tanguy, an earnest young communist Resistance fighter named Roger Cocteau, going by the Resistance name of Gallois, reached Patton's encampment with an urgent plea for help from the Colonel and the PCF. Gallois initially met a polite rebuff from Patton, awakened from a sound sleep to hear the Frenchman's statement. However, Patton soon returned with a bottle of champagne and then ordered Gallois driven to Omar Bradley's headquarters. There, Gallois repeated his pleas, embellishing them with information that von Choltitz intended to surrender as soon as the Allies arrived.

Bradley decided to send Leclerc and the 2e DB Tank

Division the next day to take Paris, but the French general had already sent an advance force of 150 men in halftracks, plus 10 armored cars and 10 light tanks, to Rambouillet under the command of Jacques de Guillebon to secure the town as a staging area for the push into Paris. Though Bradley later unfairly mocked Leclerc for "dancing" his way to Paris, the Free French and their commander showed initiative and aggression throughout the operation.

On the 22nd, Bradley himself flew to Le Mans to deliver the order to advance on Paris to Leclerc. He did so within moments of arriving, greeting Leclerc on the airfield with the words "You win. They've decided to send you straight to Paris." Within hours, the 2e DB Armored Division began mustering for the 125 mile trip to Rambouillet, followed by a 22 mile push to Paris.

Chapter 6: The Arrival of the Free French

Pictures of combat in Paris

Heavy rain fell throughout much of August 23rd as a cold front finally broke through the hot, humid pressure area dominant throughout the month up to that point. Leclerc's tanks, armored cars, and halftracks experienced great difficulties on the muddy, slick roads between their starting point near Le Mans and their first destination, Rambouillet. Nevertheless, they pressed onward, sustaining casualties as they brushed aside German units along the way. The Free French relief column consisted of 200 M4 Sherman tanks and 4,000 other vehicles, including halftracks, tank destroyers, self-propelled howitzers, and trucks. The column included 600 artillery pieces and 16,000 men. The formidable force advanced at speed, though Bradley later sent the American 4th Infantry Division after them to "hurry them on their way."

A vicious battle erupted in Paris that morning when some French police near the Grand Palais, a famed exhibition venue beside the Seine, fired at passing Germans. The Germans assembled a force and assailed the Grand Palais, deploying a pair of Tiger I tanks and two unmanned Goliath demolition vehicles against the famous structure. A Resistance officer, Claude Roy, described the Palais burning, an attack neither ordered nor approved of by von Choltitz: "[T]he firefighters arrived. Blinded by the smoke, those trapped inside ran for the basements. Some escaped, others did not. There was an odd mixture of firefighters, rescuers, Germans, and prisoners." (Neiberg, 2012, 197).

The firing and explosions set the hay stockpiled inside for circus horses alight. Though the building survived, constructed as it is out of metal girders, it suffered considerable damage. The French defenders led the frightened circus horses out of the Palais, only to see one cut down by stray bullets. Immediately, a swarm of emaciated women appeared from nearby houses carrying kitchen knives, bowls, and pails, and began frantically slicing meat off the dead horse. In just a few minutes, their desperate frenzy for food reduced the animal to a head, guts, and bones.

A modern picture of the Grand Palais

At approximately the same time, von Choltitz received a message from the Fuhrer in faraway Berlin. Typically full of bombast, the order called for the destruction of the city. Von Choltitz, who stated the order represented "mere paper, with no military value whatsoever" (Cobb, 2013, 233-234), read the following: "The defense of Paris and its bridgehead was of decisive military and political importance. Their loss would tear open the whole coastal front […] History showed that the loss of Paris meant the loss of all France. The sharpest measures must be taken against the first signs of insurrection—public execution of the ringleaders. [...] Paris must never fall into Allied hands or only as a heap of rubble."

Whatever satisfaction the Germans felt from their attack on the Grand Palais proved short-lived, as the FFI counterattacked vigorously all over the city throughout the day. Parisians hurling Molotov cocktails even managed to disable one of the terrible Tiger I tanks. The Germans, sensing the end of the occupation nearing, surrendered readily rather than fight in many locations. The Resistance seized 650 prisoners, plus 9 armored vehicles and 8 towed artillery pieces, by sunset on the 23rd.

The BBC mistakenly announced the liberation of Paris at around noon on the 23rd, prompting erroneous celebrations as far away as New York City. De Gaulle received numerous congratulatory messages from generals and heads of state, which he chose to interpret as a favorable sign for his political future.

Meanwhile, Leclerc's tanks and infantry moved out of Rambouillet towards Paris at 6:15 a.m. on August 24th. The 2e DB Armored Division pushed forward in two main columns, with a small third force pushing towards St. Cyr as a diversion. Leclerc attempted to push into the city that day, impatient to liberate the capital of France, but numerous 88mm flak gun batteries manned by German outposts slowed the French advance to a crawl. In the dense suburbs, the French could not simply go around these emplacements and found themselves forced to reduce them in detail, taking hundreds of prisoners in the process.

A picture of French soldiers from the 2e DB Armored Division fighting in Paris

A picture of civilians and Free French soldiers avoiding German sniper fire

Towards the end of the day, at Leclerc's orders, a company of Spanish Republican (communist) infantry, supported by half a dozen M2 halftracks and three M4A2 Sherman tanks under Captain Raymond Dronne, slipped into the city proper. They made their way first to the Hotel de Ville, then to the Police Prefecture. As dusk fell, von Choltitz heard the huge bells of Notre Dame begin to ring, followed by those of all the other churches and cathedrals, sending waves of metallic sound rolling over the Paris rooftops. Von Choltitz picked up his telephone and dialed the headquarters of his immediate superior, Hans Speidel. Holding up the receiver to the open window so Speidel heard the bells pealing, von Choltitz then declared simply that "the Allies have arrived."

The following morning, the 2e DB Armored Division and the U.S. 4th Infantry poured into Paris with almost no initial resistance, other than the crush of cheering, flower-throwing Parisians. Young women scrambled up onto tanks and other armored vehicles to kiss the liberators, then cheerily festooned the steel giants as they continued to creep through the streets towards the city center.

A picture of soldiers from the 4th U.S. Infantry looking at the Eiffel Tower

Also on the morning of the 25th, Oberst Hennecke of the Panzer Lehr division brought a relief and reinforcement column of the elite Panzer Lehr Division into Paris' northeastern suburbs. 10 Panzer IV and Panzer V Panthers led the way, followed by 50 SdKfz 251 halftracks brimming with heavily armed Panzergrenadiers. In Le Bourget, however, the column came under heavy attack by Resistance fighters. The French, daring the machine gun bullets sprayed by the halftracks' MG34 machine guns, threw Molotov cocktails in showers from the rooftops. The open-topped halftracks offered no protection from this attack. As screaming, dying Panzergrenadiers burst out of the leading vehicles to be cut down by Resistance rifle fire, Oberst Hennecke decided to retreat to spare the lives of his men. The retreat removed von Choltitz's final hope of reinforcements.

Chapter 7: Freedom

The crowning moment of August 25th arrived when Lieutenant Henri Karcher burst into the Hotel Meurice at the head of a squad of men. Hurling smoke grenades, they quickly took the stunned German officers prisoner. Karcher then accepted von Choltitz's surrender in his office. The scene would have been anticlimactic had not the mob outside attempted to seize von Choltitz when he emerged, obliging the German's captors to shove and batter their way through the throng to a waiting vehicle and escape.

On the morning of the 26th, Charles de Gaulle arrived in the city, laid a wreath of crimson gladiolus flowers at the Tomb of the Unknown Soldier, relit the eternal flame, and then walked – together with a vast crowd of aides and citizens – down the Champs-Elysees. This impromptu triumphal march drew sporadic sniper fire, which de Gaulle ignored utterly, winning admiration from both his countrymen and a scattering of foreign soldiers in the throng.

Pictures of de Gaulle marching through Paris on the 26th

A picture of De Gaulle at the Tomb of the Unknown Soldier

Desfile de la "Nueve" el 26 de agosto de 1944, Paris. Amado Granell conducía el Tatra 57K

Pictures of the procession on the 26ᵗʰ in Paris

The day, superbly sunny and pleasant, offered ideal conditions for the procession. Around a million people gathered along the Champs-Elysees, atop buildings, and even on street lights and in the branches of trees along the route. Many bore improvised tricolor flags. Police cars led the way, followed by four M4 Sherman medium tanks with French crews, and de Gaulle on foot behind them, surrounded by FFI fighters and a band of self-invited Jewish partisans from the Resistance.

Continuous, thunderous cheering rolled through the flag-waving, jubilant crowds as de Gaulle passed, a powerful sound audible through much of the city. De Gaulle occasionally lifted his arms in a gesture of salute to the people who, in effect, hailed him as both conqueror and liberator in this extraordinary ceremony. According to Simone de Beauvoir, "Mixed in the immense crowd, we acclaimed not a military parade, but a popular   carnival, disorganized and magnificent."

Approximately a mile from Notre Dame, de Gaulle climbed into an open-topped touring car. By 4:30 p.m., the French leader reached the famous cathedral for a celebratory mass. Once again, concealed assailants loosed bullets at the crowd of people. Malcolm Muggeridge, an English agent, described the scene in highly emotional terms: "The effect was fantastic. The huge congregation who had all been standing suddenly fell flat on their faces … There was a single exception; one solitary figure, like a lonely giant. It was, of course, de Gaulle. Thenceforth, that was how I always saw him—towering and alone; the rest, prostrate." (Horne, 2002, 349). Though de Gaulle remained unharmed, his bodyguards, prone on the ground around him, opened fire wildly at anyone on the surrounding rooftops whom they believed looked suspicious. Jean-Paul Sartre, the renowned author, barely escaped alive when bullets raked across the balcony he occupied. The Minister of Finance, watching from his office window, died instantly when FFI shots punched through his body. Six other people died, and more probably suffered unconfirmed wounds or fatal injuries. Though de Gaulle said nothing, the incident resolved him to bring the FFI to heel forthwith before more fatalities ensued. He also blamed the communists for the assassination attempt – as he classified it – and planned to rein them in as well.

At the Hotel de Ville, de Gaulle gave a rousing speech:

"Why do you wish us to hide the emotion which seizes us all, men and women, who are here, at home, in Paris that stood up to liberate itself and that succeeded in doing this with its own hands?

No! We will not hide this deep and sacred emotion. These are minutes which go beyond each of our poor lives. Paris! Paris outraged! Paris broken! Paris martyred! But Paris liberated! Liberated by itself, liberated by its people with the help of the French armies, with the support and the help of all France, of the France that fights, of the only France, of the real France, of the eternal France!

Well! Since the enemy which held Paris has capitulated into our hands, France returns to Paris, to her home. She returns bloody, but quite resolute. She returns there enlightened by the immense lesson, but more certain than ever of her duties and of her rights.

I speak of her duties first, and I will sum them all up by saying that for now, it is a matter of the duties of war. The enemy is staggering, but he is not beaten yet. He remains on our soil.

It will not even be enough that we have, with the help of our dear and admirable Allies, chased him from our home for us to consider ourselves satisfied after what has happened. We want to enter his territory as is fitting, as victors.

This is why the French vanguard has entered

Paris with guns blazing. This is why the great French army from Italy has landed in the south and is advancing rapidly up the Rhône valley. This is why our brave and dear Forces of the interior will arm themselves with modern weapons. It is for this revenge, this vengeance and justice, that we will keep fighting until the final day, until the day of total and complete victory.

This duty of war, all the men who are here and all those who hear us in France know that it demands national unity. We, who have lived the greatest hours of our History, we have nothing else to wish than to show ourselves, up to the end, worthy of France. Long live France!"

A picture of de Gaulle speaking after the liberation

De Gaulle had showed prudence by distrusting the communists, whether or not they engineered the possible attempt on his life. That same day, August 26th, many French communists gathered at 44 Rue Pelletier to discuss the possibility of a communist coup that would transform France into a Marxist totalitarian state. The three leading French communists – Charles Tillon, Benoit Franchon, and the small but cunning Jacques Duclos – met with 17 other Central Committee members to discuss the takeover idea. However, Duclos, the de facto leader thanks to his wiliness and Soviet connections, as well as his status as the second in command of the exiled deserter and PCF leader Maurice Thorez, quashed the revolutionary scheming. A simple reason lay behind Duclos' filibuster; Stalin knew clearly that his armies would only continue to advance on the Eastern Front while supplied with vast amounts of trucks, trains, weapons, ammunition, boots, and food by the United States' Lend-Lease program. In fact, over 50% of all Soviet materiel used during the war came from America, and many vital weapons systems and vehicles made in the USSR used American-supplied raw materials. Without Lend-Lease, the Wehrmacht juggernaut would very likely have crushed the Soviet Union and added it to Hitler's domain in 1942 to 1943, and if the French communists overthrew democracy in France, Stalin reasoned, this would enrage the Americans, probably to the point of cutting off Lend-Lease and leaving the Red Army potentially crippled. The Russian dictator even dreaded the possibility that a French communist insurrection would prompt the Americans to make peace with Hitler or even ally with him against the Marxists. For this reason, Duclos passed on the orders of his Muscovite overlord, halting the revolutionary impulse in its tracks. The communists remained largely passive and de Gaulle gained the breathing space necessary to establish firm, lawful control of the nation.

The Allied liberation of Paris was one of the seminal

events of World War II, but the event whitewashed reality. As the Allies were entering Paris, the Free French forces led by de Gaulle naturally wanted to lead the way. The Allies had just one problem with de Gaulle's desire: thousands of his men were black. The chief of staff for Allied Supreme Commander Eisenhower wrote to de Gaulle, "It is more desirable that the division mentioned above consist of white personnel." Indeed, the Free French forces were so diverse that there was no all-white division among the forces. At the time, the Free French forces were only 40 percent white, because they had heavily conscripted men from colonies in West Africa, forcing tens of thousands of blacks to fight for them. Now that those black men had fought and died, they were to be left out of the liberation, and the French had to segregate their divisions to create a new, all white one. Ironically, as a result, the Free French division that led the liberation of Paris was comprised of a great number of Spaniards, along with Syrians and whites from North Africa.

Chapter 8: The Aftermath

Among all the participants of the events in August 1944, with the exception of Adolf Hitler, there reigned a desire to keep Paris itself intact. All sides found a strange common ground in the wish to leave the capital of fashion and the good life undamaged, whatever else might happen. This sentiment, only natural in the Parisians themselves, found active expression in the actions of both their allies and their enemies, too. The British and American decision to bypass Paris rather than attack and liberate it by force developed partly due to supply difficulties and the focus on using the fuel available to push for the German border, added to the urgent need to reach Berlin before Stalin's Soviets. However, it also stemmed from their aversion to possibly leveling the French capital in the course of battle, destroying its monuments and famous buildings with the demolishing violence of modern warfare. American General Omar N. Bradley summarized both motivations candidly in his memoirs of the campaign: "[I]t would have been August before we could count on quantity tonnage through Cherbourg, September before we broke out. Instead of wintering on the Siegfried Line, we would have been lucky to have reached the Seine. And France rather than the Rhineland would have been ravaged during the winter campaign. But for the boldness of Eisenhower's decision, even Paris might have been reduced by artillery and air bombardment." (Bradley, 1964, 268).

It's somewhat interesting the Wehrmacht shared the Allies' reluctance to cause excessive harm to the City of Light. Their reasons showed more complexity, in that they also wished to survive a war they sensed the Allies would likely win and already had an eye on postwar war crimes charges. However, some evidence exists also that they valued the city as a human cultural heritage and saw no reason to vindictively damage it.

Driven by characteristic spite, Hitler ordered the destruction of Paris by Luftwaffe bombing and the use of V-1 and V-2 "vengeance" missiles. He also commanded the Wehrmacht to attack and retake the city, the latter an almost impossible dream with the German forces crumpling under the impact of Patton's Third Army advance. Obedient to the Fuhrer as far as their precarious situation allowed, the Luftwaffe launched a bombing raid against Paris on the evening of August 26th. The bombers of Luftflotte 3 under Generaloberst Otto Dessloch, 150 in number, struck while the Parisians wildly celebrated their liberation with drinking, dancing, music, and amorous pursuits. The raid caught the city unprepared, causing 214 deaths, wounding 914 people, and blasting 597 buildings in Paris' east into rubble, including the Halles aux Vins.

Paris escaped lightly nevertheless. With nearer airfields, Dessloch's Heinkel He-177 heavy bombers would have used shuttle bombing, with each bomber making up to 1 successive sorties to keep up a conveyor belt of ruin on the luckless target. 10 times as many bombs would have killed far more and leveled a considerable area of the City of Light. Additionally, the Germans found themselves unable to bring the V-1 and V-2 batteries to bear, a single volley six days later on September 1st killing just six people.

Hitler had ordered the French capital burned, but von Choltitz, the man on the scene, may have refused to comply. Though some historians believe this to be self-serving revisionism by Choltitz, it is fairly certain that some of his officers talked him out of airstrikes near Notre Dame due to concern that it might be damaged.

In the days after the liberation, bands of Germans still held out in various places around the city. A shocking confirmation of this came when 2,600 German soldiers emerged from the Bois de Boulogne shortly after de Gaulle passed it. Fortunately for the French, these heavily-armed men merely wished to surrender. Other pockets of German resistance gave way on the 26th, with most surrenders accepted by both the French and the Americans. Resistance fighters butchered a few prisoners in the aftermath of the victory, often despite the objections of their comrades in arms, but most of the Germans who surrendered received relatively decent treatment. After interrogation, the Americans sent them to rear area POW camps until the war ended.

A picture of German POWs in Paris

The last fighting took place at the Paris airport on August 28th, 1944. The Germans showed one last flare-up of the Wehrmacht fighting spirit, but in vain, as a *Daily Mail* article from August 30th described: "The desperation and hopelessness of German resistance is typified by the battle for Le Bourget aerodrome. For six hours, German troops fought fanatically for this 'Croyden' Paris. The battle took place after German infantry had rejected a surrender ultimatum by French forces. The enemy had three defence lines, but no heavy armour or artillery and they were butchered by the French tanks. They asked for no quarter in this one-sided battle…Some Germans jumped on top of a tank and dropped hand grenades inside."

No significant German forces ever again approached Paris during the war. Patton's advance and the equally powerful attack from the south by the Operation Cobra forces ended the Wehrmacht's effective presence in France within 7 to 8 days of the airport battle, and only lack of fuel prevented a drive into Germany during early autumn.

The liberation of Paris brought another victory parade to the Champs-Élysées in the waning days. Many Free French soldiers who conducted a victory parade down the Champs-Élysées on August 26 were likely familiar with the avenues, but Paris would have been new for most of the young men in the U.S. Army's 28th Infantry Division, which were greeted as liberators on August 29. During the victory parade, the Americans were immersed in Paris' history, beauty, high culture, and the residents' pride in their city and history. Though the American soldiers were probably unaware, the Champs-Élysées that they paraded down had been greatly expanded a few generations earlier; what was once a narrow road full of gardens and groves in the 19th century had become a wide avenue outlined with perfect symmetry by trees on each side. By then, the Champs-Élysées had the garden-filled square of

Carré Marigny bordering it, which remains an open air market today and an example of the green spaces designed in Georges-Eugène Haussmann's urban planning.

The Americans marched past plenty of small shops that could have escaped attention, but they couldn't miss the Grand Palais, which reflected the neoclassical architecture of the late 19th century known as Beaux-Arts, but much of the architecture still on the Champs-Élysées during the victory parade was Baroque, reflecting Paris' history. The 28th Division would also have noticed the Théâtre Marigny, a panoramic theatre that often housed musicals and film before and after the war.

As with the Nazi victory parade in June 1940, the parades made their way to the magnificent Arc de Triomphe, Napoleon's monument to his own victories. Along with the Tomb of the Unknown Soldier, the Arc is dedicated to French veterans of the French Revolution and Napoleonic wars, along with the names of the battles inscribed on it. One of the city's most recognizable monuments, the Arc stands in the middle of the "Axe historique," or historical axis," the square designed by Haussmann whose roads lead to some of the city's most historic monuments and museums. However, the 28th Division could not march the entire axis, which includes landmarks like the Louvre and new ones like the Grande Arche of La Défense, a huge arch that stands guard over

Paris' main financial district. Though the Parisians didn't realize it, the Americans were making their way north to fight the retreating Germans that same day, and the victory parade was part of a battle march.

Picture of the U.S. 28th Infantry division marching through Paris

With the Germans defeated and driven from the city or taken prisoner, the Parisians turned to exacting revenge on real or alleged collaborators, and many took advantage of the anarchy to denounce their personal rivals and enemies as collaborators in order to draw the general ire down upon them. Dubbed the "Epuration Sauvage" or "Savage

Purge," this period began in August and continued through September.

For his part, de Gaulle deplored the anarchic, vindictive violence, and he worked to restore order quickly, but weeks passed before systematic application of the rule of law began in earnest in the liberated city. During that time, thousands of people died as a result of lynch mobs, and tens of thousands suffered lesser penalties. De Gaulle appealed to his fellow citizens in a radio broadcast: "It is true that many made mistakes at one moment or the other, since this thirty years' war broke out in 1914…Let us try to forget! France is made up of all Frenchmen. Unless she is to perish, she needs the hearts, the spirits and the strength of all her sons and daughters." (De Gaulle, 1960, 130).

However, few heeded these words, and a miniature Reign of Terror succeeded the Germans' defeat. Often chosen on the flimsiest pretexts or rumors and given no trial or opportunity to defend themselves, these victims of mob justice served as scapegoats. Those "punishing" them frequently shared just as much "guilt" in collaborating with the Germans (accepting wages from them, for example), but they hypocritically demonized the chosen victims to purge their own sense of guilt.

Men accused of collaboration frequently suffered

murderous attacks, shot to death in their homes, in darkened alleys, or in ditches outside the city. A mob seized one noted Resistance fighter after people initially mistook his telescope for a rifle and threw him to his death under the tracks of a passing Sherman tank. Hundreds and perhaps as many as several thousands of Parisians – mostly male but also female, frequently chosen almost at random – were killed by unofficial death squads during the Epuration Sauvage.

After the liberation, the FFI took over the Nazi-built Drancy Internment Camp, located in a Paris suburb, and by using arbitrary arrests of actual and assumed collaborators, the FFI gathered at least 4,000 prisoners at Drancy. The behavior of the French guards differed little from that of the SS personnel who recently vacated the camp. One of the prisoners later reported that the internees found themselves "at the mercy of forty FFI. These were commanded by a young chief of twenty-two, himself liberated from Drancy and animated with the single spirit of retaliation … Numerous women have been violated. Many internees were woken up at night and beaten until blood flowed." (Horne, 2002, 351). Indeed, the ritual abuse of tens of thousands of women formed a very prominent feature of the Epuration Sauvage. Though cloaked under the excuse of punishing those guilty of "horizontal collaboration" –engaging in sexual relations with Germans during the occupation – careful research in recent years revealed that at least half of the women did not suffer ritual degradation for this reason.

Mobs of men selected certain women as victims and shaved their heads in public. The men also stripped many of these women partially or wholly naked and forced them to parade through the streets in this state, photographing the spectacle for publication. Sometimes, the mob used paint to mark the faces, breasts, or buttocks of the women with swastikas.

Most of the women escaped with no more harm than a period of public humiliation with sexual overtones. Some, however, also suffered beatings, torture, mutilation, or rape. The mobs beat or kicked a handful of women to death while parading them through the streets. Occasionally, some of the women expressed defiance towards their tormenters, as in the case of one who shouted angrily at the men shaving her head, "My ass is international, but my heart is French."

Assigning guilt for the death of someone murdered years before by the Gestapo always provided an excuse for loosing sadistic impulses on a human target: "Jean Cocteau records being shocked by the sight of one woman, "completely naked," on the Avenue de la Grande Armée: "they tore at her, they pushed her, they pulled her, they spat in her face. Her head had been shaven. She was covered in bruises and carried around her neck a placard: 'I had my husband shot.'" (Horne, 2002, 350).

The mobs appeared motivated by a strong undercurrent of misogyny and an effort to reestablish male dominance. Women comprised the vast majority of accusers who picked out targets, frequently aiming mobs towards other women with better economic success than themselves. Men exempted all sex workers from vengeance, claiming that prostitutes could not be blamed for accepting any customer, even a German. In doing so, of course, they ensured the availability of non-disfigured sex workers for their own use.

The special type of hatred directed at women seemed, at times, rooted in resentment of their prominent role in both the Resistance and the Liberation as combatants, organizers, messengers, and spies. An inchoate desire to "put women in their place again" groped for expression through the ritual degradation inflicted on at least 16,000 Parisian women, just as the Vichy regime mobilized the support of conservative social elements by attempting (mainly ineffectually) to quash women's rights.

Ultimately, the disapproval of foreign observers proved more effective than de Gaulle's stirring speeches about unity at mitigating the Epuration Sauvage. "American,

Canadian, and British soldiers, especially, found the practice repugnant, and at times they would interfere to protect the victims; we have reports, letters, and

interviews with them in which they show how much respect they had lost for the French. All this soon pushed the practice and its recording onto a back burner as the French tried to regain the moral upper hand." (Rosbottom, 2014, 279).

Nevertheless, the process continued at a lower level, only gradually dying out as de Gaulle established new legal and police authority on the ruins of the Vichy government. A fresh flare-up occurred briefly in mid-1945 following the end of the war and the liberation of prison camp inmates. The government carried out its own purge – the Epuration Legale – but actually used standards of evidence and trials in most cases. These proceedings led to 991 executions, as opposed to the thousands killed during the Epuration Sauvage across all of France.

Eventually, Paris grew politically free again and once more sought to become the capital of fashion, ebullience, and joyous living. That said, the occupation left a mark the liberation failed to erase. Expelling the Germans did not mean resuming business as usual; the memory of Vichy, the sacrifice of France's Jews, and the vicious excesses of the Epuration Sauvage lingered. Hitler's brief dominion over France held up a mirror in which the City of Light saw, with reluctant clarity, the darkness lurking within itself.

Of course, the liberation also had a much lighter side, one which the Americans and later British savored to the full alongside the newly freed French. Though de Gaulle's political experiment eventually failed, leading to a changed French Republic, and many other problems and opportunities developed in the following years, the French and their liberators – both native and foreign – found the opportunity to express a holiday mood alive with hope missing during years of danger, occupation, and war. One individual in Paris at the time wrote, "There is joy in the air. The boulevards and the Champs-Elysees are back to their bustling selves. Different types of Allied aeroplane fly over the capital endlessly. […] There is still no gas, no electricity, no Metro. It doesn't matter! This is the first relaxed Sunday of the Liberation. Paris has been given back to us. Paris is coming back to life." (Cobb, 2013, 344).

In all, the liberation of Paris represented a remarkable achievement in World War II. The city of 2.5 million gained its freedom with minimal damage and emerged from its trials nearly as gracious and culturally rich as it entered them. 20,000 Germans surrendered for a loss of only about 642 2nd Armored Division killed and wounded and the deaths of somewhat less than a thousand FFI fighters and supporters. It can certainly be said that the French Resistance and General Leclerc paid a very low cost indeed to win back one of the crown jewels of Western civilization.

Online Resources

Other World War II titles by Charles River Editors

Other titles about Nazi Germany by Charles River Editors

Bibliography

Argyle, Ray. The Paris Game: Charles de Gaulle, the Liberation of Paris, and the Gamble that   Won France. Ontario, 2014.

Beevor, Anthony, and Artemis Cooper. Paris After the Liberation. London, 2007.

Bradley, Omar N. A Soldier's Story. New York, 1964.

Cobb, Matthew. Eleven Days in August: The Liberation of Paris in 1944. London, 2013.

De Gaulle, Charles. The War Memoirs of Charles de Gaulle, Volume 2. New York, 1960.

Horne, Alistair. Seven Ages of Paris. New York, 2002.

Kaplan, Bernard. "The Swede Who 'Saved Paris' From Germans." The Milwaukee Journal,   Saturday, May

10th, 1958, page 8.

Mitcham, Samuel W. Retreat to the Reich: the German Defeat in France, 1944. Westport, 2000.

Mitchell, Allan. Nazi Paris: the History of an Occupation, 1940-1944. London, 2008.

Neiberg, Michael. The Blood of Free Men: the Liberation of Paris, 1944. New York, 2012.

Rosbottom, Ronald C. When Paris Went Dark: the City of Light Under German Occupation,   1940-1944. New York, 2014.

Tully, Andrew. Berlin: The Story of a Battle. Lake Oswego, 2013. (Digital edition.)

Zaloga, Steven J. Liberation of Paris 1944: Patton's Race for the Seine. Oxford, 2008.

Made in the USA
Monee, IL
06 February 2022

90769787R00057